# THE HEYDAY OF THE
# LONDON BUS – 3

## Kevin McCormack

IAN ALLAN
*Publishing*

First published 1996

ISBN 0 7110 2486 3

© Kevin McCormack 1996

Published by Ian Allan Publishing

an imprint of Ian Allan Ltd,
Terminal House, Station Approach,
Shepperton, Surrey TW17 8AS.
Printed by Ian Allan Printing Ltd,
Coombelands House, Coombelands Lane,
Addlestone, Surrey KT15 1HY.

*Front cover:*
**Endangered species**
LT's Leyland Tigers were close to extinction
when TD87 was caught at Cobham on 22 July
1961. Although only four years older than the RFs
which replaced them, the TDs belonged to a
different era and were the last Central Area
buses with crash gearboxes. This scene is easily
re-created today because Cobham Bus Museum's
superbly restored TD95 lives just down the road.
*Gerald Mead*

*Title page:*
**Watch the birdie**
With cap in hand and Gibson ticket machine at
the ready, RT3238's conductor poses for the
camera at Tring in July 1969. Within six months,
LT's presence in this area, as symbolised by the
famous bullseye motif, would disappear for ever.
*Dave Brown*

*Right:*
**Final countdown**
Nearly 24 years of trolleybus operation between
Holborn and North Finchley is coming to an end.
With just three days to go, No 1487 crosses New
Southgate bridge on 4 November 1961.
*Hugh Ramsey*

# Introduction

Following the interest shown in the first two colour albums, I am pleased to present a third *Heyday of the London Bus*.

With the disposal of London's central and suburban bus services to a variety of operators, we have seen the biggest shake-up since the demise of the independents and the creation of London Transport (LT) in 1933. The bus wheels have turned full circle, but at least the traditional red livery largely survives, as do many of the famous bus routes.

Even greater change has occurred in the Country area. Reminders of LT's tenure, which ended over 25 years ago, are few and far between: mainly some old concrete bus stops with fading red or green caps, or the occasional tubular bus shelter. Most of the substantial brick garages of the 1930s have gone and today's vehicles now carry strange liveries. Many familiar routes have disappeared and their numbers now turn up in unexpected places, such as Clapham Junction.

Yet the past is not forgotten. Routemasters have overtaken the RT's seemingly unassailable record of 40 years of public service and look set to take Londoners into the next century. Lincoln green has returned to the Country area as representatives of the RM, RT, RF and GS classes appear on special services. Then there are the preserved bus rallies to visit, and the museums with their excellent LT collections: Covent Garden, Cobham and Carlton Colville. Private preservation of LT vehicles has certainly moved on apace since tramcar No 1858 started the wheels rolling in 1952.

## Acknowledgements

In compiling this book, I have drawn on many sources of information, but I must mention in particular the superb LOTS journal, *The London Bus Magazine*, and the *RT Story* by Ken Blacker.

On the photographic side I am most grateful once again to Geoff Rixon, Dick Riley, Jim Collins, Steve Fennell and C. Carter (to whom particular thanks must go for the use of what may be the only prewar colour photograph of a London bus), and to Bill Ballard for his help. I also have some new contributors to thank: Mike Harries, Dave Brown, Hugh Ramsey and Gerald Mead. The photographers have, between them, provided a considerable variety of vehicle types, from the favourite standards to some of the less successful designs of the late 1960s and 1970s which nevertheless attract a following. The material also covers a wide time span, from 1939 to LT's 50th anniversary in 1983. Who would have imagined then that there would be no more LT jubilees or that Chiswick and Aldenham works would be no more?

On that sad note, it's time to start turning the pages for a nostalgic journey through London and its countryside.

*Kevin R. McCormack*
*Ashtead*
*Surrey*
*January 1996*

*Left:*

**Heavy load**
Most of the 72 seats in RML2456 appear to be taken in this view near Uxbridge on 6 May 1978. London Country inherited 209 Routemaster buses and coaches from LT on its formation in 1970, but the total elimination of conductor-operated buses limited their lifespan with the company to just 10 years. On realising that scrapping had started, LT promptly bought back the remainder. *Geoff Rixon*

*Above:*
**Thames crossing**
RT1524 samples the delights of Richmond on its journey from Highgate (Archway station) in June 1964. 'Via' blinds with capital letters were being phased out by this time. *Mike Harries*

*Opposite:*
**Vanishing cream**
The relentless march towards 100% one-person operation (OPO) in the Country Area is already under way in this June 1969 view of Merlin MBS272 leading Daimler Fleetline XF7 through Reigate. This shot serves as a reminder that it was London Transport rather than its successor, London Country, that introduced yellow into the green livery to replace the long-established cream colour. The former East Surrey garage, now demolished can be seen on the left. *Mike Harries*

*Opposite:*
**Q-riosity**
This futuristic machine, with side-mounted engine, full front and side entrance (not visible here), was once Q4, one of only five LT double-deck AEC Qs. Q4 entered service at Leatherhead garage in the summer of 1934, but the type was withdrawn in 1939, being too advanced for its time. After wartime storage, Q4 was sold to G. H. Ennifer Ltd (Blue Ensign) of Doncaster, where it is recorded here on 19 September 1950. The phoney grille fitted by its new owner is a possible attempt to reassure passengers that this is a normal bus with the engine at the front. *C. Carter*

*Above:*
**War paint**
It is August 1939 and painted kerb stones, white-tipped mudguards and masked headlamps signify the impending blackout. The scene is the Crown at Loughton, where two LTs of 1929 vintage, from the first batch of 150 built with outside staircases, are waiting to set off for Victoria on route 38a. Ten years later, LTs such as these brought an end to outside staircase operation on regular service. *C. Carter*

*Left:*
**Metamorphosis**
The RF underfloor-engined coach served Green Line from 1951 until 1979, an extraordinary achievement in view of the demanding duties it was required to perform. An expansion of services in the mid-1950s brought a requirement for additional vehicles and the existing Green Line fleet of 263 RFs was augmented by the conversion into coaches of six Central Area and 19 Country Area buses. One of the latter, ex-RF525, is seen here at Hertford on 16 September 1961 in its new guise as RF306. The renumbering was to keep the Green Line coaches in numerical sequence. *Hugh Ramsey*

*Below left:*
**Out of favour**
The RT family numbered nearly 7,000 vehicles, of which Leyland RTLs and RTWs accounted for some 2,100. When a start was made on replacing the fleet in the 1960s, the less popular Leylands were targeted first. Stockwell garage lost its RTL allocation in August 1967 and four months earlier RTL1436 was caught on camera near Mitcham. *Geoff Rixon*

*Opposite:*
**Fallen star**
RM1, heralded as 'London's Bus of the Future' when it made its début at the 1954 Commercial Motor Show, ran for only three years in public service before being transferred to training duties. In 1973 it was even sold, becoming a mobile test bed for the Lockheed Hydraulic Brake Co, but was later reacquired by LT for preservation. When RM1 first appeared it had a rather unattractive front end which resulted from the fitting of an underfloor radiator to keep the vehicle within existing length restrictions (27ft 6in). When the limit was increased to 30ft, the radiator was mounted at the front and a grille fitted. RM1 is seen here at East Twickenham in May 1967. *Geoff Rixon*

*Opposite:*
**Modern Times**
This is a typical 1970s urban scene dominated by rear-engined double-deckers and high rise office blocks. The location is West Croydon and the date is St Patrick's Day 1977. London Country was desperately short of buses and hired a motley assortment, including five crew-operated Atlanteans from Maidstone Borough Council. No 35, dating from 1967, stands beside AN37, one of 90 Park Royal-bodied Atlanteans. *Jim Collins*

*Above:*
**Ship ahoy**
As well as hiring buses, London Country also purchased some strange vehicles, including three ex-Southdown Leyland PD3/5s (nicknamed Queen Marys) which dated from 1961/62. These were pressed into service at Godstone garage without so much as a repaint. Ex-Southdown No 933 travels along Coulsdon Road on 6 January 1976. *Jim Collins*

*Left:*
**Homing device**
RTW368, belying its 8ft width in this view, displays the scanning indicator plate between the decks which was fitted to buses on certain routes in an early attempt at electronic bus control. By August 1965, when this photograph was taken at Marble Arch, the RTW class had been decimated and the last survivors ran in public service the following May. *Geoff Rixon*

*Opposite:*
**Early riser**
Low bridge RLHs never operated in central London and, therefore, it was a surprise to find Dalston's RLH29 parked at Farringdon at 8am on 28 August 1964. Like several of the class, RLH29 subsequently emigrated, albeit relatively recently, and has joined RLHs Nos 24 and 35 in Basle, Switzerland.
*Hugh Ramsey*

*Right:*
**Surplus to requirements**
RT4758 was one of 144 unwanted RTs and RTLs completed in 1954 and stored for the next four years because the expected growth in bus services did not materialise. Indeed these vehicles only found work through the disposal of earlier RTs and RTLs. RT4758 entered service in March 1958 and is seen in August 1969 in the attractive village of Framlingham in Kent.
*Dave Brown*

*Opposite:*
**National institution**
This term is as relevant to the bus as it is to the art gallery behind, since the Routemaster is in its fifth decade of public service in London and should easily reach the Millennium. In October 1969, RML2568 heads across the north side of Trafalgar Square, bearing witness to those pre-decimalisation and pre-metrication days.
*Mike Harries*

*Opposite:*
**Fading light**
Only three months of RT operation on route 102 remain as RT219, numerically one of the earliest still in operation at this date, picks up passengers at Golders Green on 29 December 1977. *Jim Collins*

*Above:*
**Select few**
Whereas LT bought over 2,500 Daimler Fleetlines, London Country made do with just 11, preferring the Leyland Atlantean as its standard rear-engined double-decker. AF10 crosses Coulsdon Common on 27 June 1976. *Jim Collins*

*Above:*
**No way up**
In 1975/76, London Country acquired 20 ex-Ribble Leyland Titan PD3/4s and then removed the staircases (which were located behind the driver) in order to use the buses as trainers. LR2 visits Surbiton on 11 May 1978. *Geoff Rixon*

*Opposite:*
**All change**
Apart from the ubiquitous London taxis, this scene outside Charing Cross station on 25 March 1974 is very different today. Green Volvos now operate the 176; the building on the left has been replaced by a glass atrium totally out of keeping with the Nash façade (see page 29 of the first album) and Rhodesia House in the background is now Zimbabwe House. Any offers for RT2063's numberplate? *R. C. Riley*

*Opposite:*
**Silver lady**
Following a similar
experiment on the
Underground, LT
ordered one unpainted
Routemaster (RM664)
to test the endurance of
aluminium surfaces.
The vehicle was tried
out at various garages
over 3½ years until its
appearance
deteriorated and it was
painted red. RM664
was operating from
Fulwell garage when
photographed at
Heathrow in September
1964. *Mike Harries*

*Left:*
**Beneath Box Hill**
Burford Bridge, near
Mickleham, in October
1965 sees RF182
making its way from
Dorking to Luton, via
Baker Street, on Green
Line route 714.
*Mike Harries*

*Right:*

**Long service award**
RMC4, formerly CRL4 dating from 1957, was the only one of the four prototype Routemasters to enjoy a normal lifespan in passenger service. Standing at Hatfield in September 1973, RMC4 has probably reached its nadir in terms of appearance, particularly with its chalked route number, but the vehicle was to last almost to the end of London Country RM operation. Fortunately, its contribution to history was recognised and following withdrawal in May 1979 this unique RM was quickly restored to its Green Line glory for special duties.
*Mike Harries*

*Opposite:*

**Risen from the ashes**
Elmers End garage was destroyed by a flying bomb in 1944. Here it is in rebuilt form on 19 May 1973, when it was host to RTs Nos 4539, 2972, 2278 and 1648 as well as RM417. The latter was one of only a hundred Routemasters to wear the short-lived open bullseye symbol.
*R. C. Riley*

*Above:*
**School bus**
For the best part of 24 years, the RFs had the monopoly of the single-deck routes in the Kingston area, but the mid-1970s saw their gradual replacement, mainly by Bristol LHs (designated the BL class). The photographer, under the watchful eye of his son, captures BL48 in Station Road, Thames Ditton, in September 1980, the last month of operation of route 201. BLs remained in service with LT until 1990. *Geoff Rixon*

*Opposite:*
**Window dressing**
A clever design to give passengers excellent viewing facilities was not matched by success in the mechanical department. The result was that the SMA class, comprising 21 AEC Swift chassis originally ordered by South Wales Transport and diverted to London Country in 1972, lasted only six years in Green Line service. SMA13 is pictured at Hampton Court on 11 March 1978 passing the delightful Craven House, a building once occupied by Ian Allan Ltd. *Geoff Rixon*

*Opposite:*
**Off his trolley**
The driver was obviously in a hurry to abandon his charge, a 1936-built Leyland, in Forest Road, Walthamstow on 3 June 1950. In the background is a mid-1930s bus shelter, examples of which can still be seen today in locations as diverse as Trafalgar Square (Duncannon Street) and Reigate. *C. Carter*

*Above:*
**Independent survivor**
Although the City Motor Omnibus Co had to relinquish its London routes to the LPTB in 1934, it retained its Southend-Wood Green service which ran until 1981, latterly as Eastern National route 251. On 3 June 1950, City No D4, a year-old lowbridge Daimler CVD6, drops passengers in Eastern Avenue, Gants Hill. The slogan on the bus has a certain irony today! *C. Carter*

*Above:*

**Country splendour**

St Alban's garage upholds LT's tradition of impeccably presented buses, as evidenced by this line-up of RTs Nos 3249, 2369 and 3891 alongside RF546 on 20 May 1968. RT2369 is contemplating a 'short' Green Line working to Victoria of the 713 Dunstable-Dorking service. *Hugh Ramsey*

*Opposite:*

**Getting a wetting**

RT3949 has received a well-earned wash at Bexleyheath garage on 25 March 1978. Dating from 1935, this was the only purpose-built trolleybus depot (the remainder being converted from tram use) and was unlucky to suffer two bomb attacks during the war. *Geoff Rixon*

29

*Above:*

**Double firsts**

XA1 and FRM1 stand at West Croydon bus station in June 1970. The unique front-entrance, rear-engined Routemaster is working the Central Area's first double-deck OPO route (No 233). The vehicle contained 60% of standard RM components and, like the XAs, had a combined entrance/exit. FRM1 worked alongside the XAs until they were sold to Hong Kong in 1973. *Mike Harries*

*Opposite:*

**Reluctant inheritance**

Almost 18 months into London Country's existence, ex-LT vehicles still dominate the forecourt at Chelsham garage. Centre stage is occupied by former Green Line coach, RF153, now demoted to bus work but fulfilling its old role here. Among the phalanx of RTs is former Green Line RT620 with pale green central relief band and, to the right, RTs Nos 3256 and 3136. *Mike Harries*

*Above:*

**Merlin misery**

One of LT's problem classes was the AEC Merlin, seen in green livery on page 5 and here in red at Walthamstow station. A total of 665 of these vehicles were bought by LT between 1966 and 1969, but the length (36ft) caused overhang difficulties. LT therefore switched to the shorter AEC Swift, but this model's small engine caused even worse problems. It was left to old soldiers, such as RT4704 standing behind MB386 in this September 1975 shot, to keep the passengers moving. *Dave Brown*

*Opposite:*

**Slipping standards**

The state of RF122 at Dorking garage in July 1975 epitomises the decline into which London Country and the prestigious Green Line coach services were sliding at the time. However, after a period of oblivion, the Green Line name once more adorns the sides of London-bound coaches and at Embankment some even use a surviving LT coach stop like the one shown here. Attractive dwellings now occupy this site. *Mike Harries*

GREEN LINE
703 LONDON
(BAKER STREET)

PAY AS YOU ENTER
PLEASE

GREEN LINE

LYF 473

CAFE

COACH STOP
703 714

33

*Left:*
**Early obsolescence**
In 1953, the 84-strong GS class was introduced to replace the Leyland Cubs on minor Country Area routes. With the front end of a Fordson Thames truck and sliding windows, these Guy Vixens were very different from standard LT vehicles. Although two lasted 19 years, some were redundant within four, mainly due to a preference for the larger capacity RF. GS5 negotiates the narrow streets of Hertford on 16 September 1961. *Hugh Ramsey*

*Below left:*
**Welsh dresser**
Due to chassis production outstripping body building, LT had to look beyond its normal suppliers for help. An unusual choice was the Saunders Engineering & Shipyard Co of Beaumaris on the Isle of Anglesey, a company which clad 300 standard AEC running units with bodies of almost identical appearance to the obsolete roofbox RTs. Indeed, the only noticeable difference was the positioning of the offside number stencil, set back from the lower deck windows, as seen in this view of RT1288 at East Molesey in April 1962. *Geoff Rixon*

*Opposite:*
**Swan song**
While working in May 1967 at the Maida Vale flat of the US pop group, the Walker Brothers, the photographer decided to take his lunch break outside in order to find some fast disappearing RTLs. He was rewarded by the sight of RTL1152, in fair condition apart from a missing radiator badge. *Geoff Rixon*

*Above:*

**Swedish influence**

A resplendent RF445 from Edgware garage stands outside the Grade II listed Underground station at Arnos Grove in November 1972. The building is a typically striking design by Charles Holden, its drum shape reputedly being based on Stockholm public library. *Dave Brown*

*Opposite:*

**Last winter**

RT3715 heads into Farnborough on its journey from Woolwich, six months before the conversion of route 51 to RM operation in June 1976. *Dave Brown*

*Opposite:*

**In the hot seat**

The driver takes advantage of RLH35's opening windscreen as he waits at Woking in June 1969. In this view the angular shape of the body and the tall radiator (accentuated by the vehicle's low height) create an archaic appearance reminiscent of the STL class and in complete contrast to the rounded shape of the RT family. *Dave Brown*

*Above:*

**RM enigma**

The unique front-entrance/engined long Routemaster, which never turned a wheel in normal LT service, stands at Heathrow in September 1964. After making its début at the 1962 Commercial Motor Show, RMF1254 was loaned to other operators before joining the BEA fleet, where it pioneered the concept of towing luggage trailers. As a result, 65 similar, but shorter RMs were built, replacing the fleet of 1½-deck AEC Regal IV coaches, two of which are seen on the left. In November 1966, RML1254 was sold to Northern General, joining its fleet of 50 similar RMs. It was withdrawn in October 1980 and bought for preservation. *Mike Harries*

*Right:*
**Dashing to Dunstable**
Modernised RF163, one of 175 Green Line coaches so treated in 1966/67, hurries along the A24 near Mickleham, Surrey, in September 1968.
*Mike Harries*

*Opposite:*
**Late night final**
Heathrow Airport witnesses the end of RT operation on the 140 on 14 July 1978, leaving only three RT-operated routes running. Interestingly, back in 1951 it was RTWs and not older buses that the RTs replaced, following the lifting of the ban on the use of RTWs in central London.
*Steve Fennell*

*Opposite:*
**Last knockings**
This phrase could well sum up the mechanical condition of RF221, the penultimate London Country RF in passenger service, which expired around the time of this photograph (October 1978). Also seen here at Chelsham are RT981, recently transferred to training duties, and RMC1504, facing imminent withdrawal. *Author's collection*

*Above:*
**Superbus**
Hardly an appropriate epithet for AEC's final, and possibly most unsuccessful product, although the Swifts shown here did clock up nearly nine years on the special Stevenage service before withdrawal. June 1971 sees brand-new SMs Nos 495 and 499 at Dorking garage, resplendent in Oxford blue and canary yellow, waiting to join Nos 496-498 at Stevenage. *Mike Harries*

*Above:*
**Rose among thorns**
A shaft of sunlight illuminates RT4347 as it stands among the shadowy DMSs in Barking garage on New Year's Day 1979. London's last RT-operated route has only just over three months left to run. *Author*

*Opposite:*
**Change of programme**
The familiar sight of trolleybuses passing Finchley Odeon would end three days after this photograph was taken on 4 November 1961. North Finchley was the only trolleybus terminus in London to have routes arriving from three different directions and at peak hours there were almost 60 trolleybus departures per hour. *Hugh Ramsey*

*Opposite:*
**Royal Variety Show**
RT deliveries were not making much progress and RTLs and RTWs had not even appeared, when this assortment of vehicles was photographed on 25 April 1948 at the Royal Forest Hotel, Chingford. From left to right the buses are a Park Royal-bodied Guy Arab, a 'Camel Back' AEC Renown with body originally from one of the batch of LTs numbered 501-850, a brown-liveried Guy Arab with Massey Bros body, another Renown with bodywork from the LT851-950 series and a 'Bluebird' LT with overhanging top deck. *C. Carter*

*Above:*
**Inaugural service**
Leyland's 8ft wide RTWs first hit the streets in May 1949 on Tottenham garage's route 41. RTW25 stands at Ley Street, Ilford, on 3 June 1950, its restricted blind display serving as a reminder of wartime privations. *C. Carter*

*Right:*

**No relief**

RT620, one of 85 RTs painted in Green Line livery as back-up for the RF fleet, finds normal bus work in May 1969 at Boxhill. Route 470 started life as the 107 in 1914, bringing the General's red buses into Dorking. Following the 1924 renumbering exercise, it became route 70 and, unusually, was jointly operated by red and green buses. This practice ceased in 1938 when the northern terminus was switched from Morden to Warlingham and the service became Country Area route 470.
*Mike Harries*

*Opposite:*

**Trials and tribulations**

Seen here at Tottenham Court Road in January 1966, XA9 represents the 50-strong fleet of Park Royal-bodied Leyland Atlanteans which were the first doored double-deckers to run in London in any quantity. The XAs entered service on route 24 in 1965 and were tested against RMLs. However, the Atlanteans were frequently out of service and not surprisingly, the RMLs proved superior.
*Geoff Rixon*

*Opposite:*
**Classic lines**
LT's standard single-decker of the 1950s and 1960s, the 700-strong RF class, replaced all the prewar single-deckers except the Leyland Cubs. Standing on the railway bridge at Sutton station in March 1976 is RF530, one of 225 RFs built for bus use in the Central Area. *Dave Brown*

*Above:*
**Turning on the box**
It is easy to forget that today's plethora of road markings originated in the 1960s. Here, lowbridge RLH47 enters a box junction in Guildford in June 1969. Eventually, this fine vehicle was to meet its end in Hawaii, after being crushed by a tree. *Dave Brown*

*Opposite:*
**Air force**
Biggin Hill Air Display was noted for the fleet of extra buses used to bring passengers to this popular event. On 20 September 1969, four Country Area RTs prepare to resume their duties on route 410 to Bromley North station. *Mike Harries*

*Above:*
**Ageless expatriate**
Unlike its double-deck counterpart, the equally revolutionary Q type single-decker enjoyed nearly 20 years of service with LT, until replaced by RFs in 1952/53. Looking deceptively young for a 29-year-old, Q103 sunbathes in Malta in April 1964. This spruce veteran boasts new wheel arches, but, for an AEC, has suffered the ultimate indignity of being fitted with a Bedford grille. This covers the air intake, evidence that the vehicle was once a Green Line coach. *Mike Harries*

*Left:*
**Outboxed**
The first 749 postwar RTs had either Park Royal or Weymann bodies with roof number boxes. One such body is seen here at Richmond mounted on RT3557. At this time (June 1964), these RTs were being rapidly displaced by Routemasters following the end of the trolleybus conversion programme.
*Mike Harries*

*Opposite:*
**Traditional standards**
What a contrast there is between yesterday's staid livery of Lincoln green with cream relief and today's garish stripes that pervade many of London's country and suburban areas. RF568 serves as a reminder of those halcyon days as it sets off from Reigate in August 1969.
*Mike Harries*

*Right:*

**Stock exchange**

Although the eight XF class Daimler Fleetlines introduced in 1965 spent most of their lives in the Country Area at East Grinstead, they did venture into new territories when LT indulged in bus swopping. In its early days, the entire class visited the Central Area twice for exchange trials with the XA class Leyland Atlanteans, which were fitted with similar Park Royal bodywork. On the first visit, XF2 is seen in Highgate in May 1966. Later on, between 1969 and 1972, XFs Nos 6-8 operated in Stevenage on the new 'Blue Arrow' services, for which they were repainted in a striking blue and silver livery. Three red XAs were provided in exchange. *Geoff Rixon*

*Opposite:*

**Golden oldie**

Appropriately numbered RM1983 was nearly 20 years old when it was specially painted to commemorate the 50th anniversary of LT's formation in 1933. It is pictured here at Waterloo on 14 May 1983 while allocated to the former 'Tilling Catford' (TC) garage. This designation served as a reminder of the pre-LT period of private operators such as Thomas Tilling. RM1983 subsequently became surplus to requirements and worked in Scotland before settling in Carlisle. *Geoff Rixon*

601 LONDON'S LAST TROLLEYBUSES 8 May 1962

Commemorating London's Trolleybuses 1931 to 1962

WATCH YOUR STEP

LONDON'S LAST TROLLEYBUSES 8 May 1962

LONDON TRANSPORT

FXH 521

LONDON ROAD

FAREBROTHER & Co
INTERMENT OR CREMATION PRIVATE CHAPELS
Estd 1856
Telephone KINGSTON 3223.

F.BROTHER & Co

213 SUTTON GARAGE MALDEN WORCESTER PK

JAGUAR RECOMMEND CASTROL

MXX 479

536 VPL

*Opposite:*
**Hail and Farewell**
London's trolleybuses started in the Kingston area and that is where they ended, 31 years later. With no crash helmets or 'go-faster' stripes in sight, two policemen on their Velocettes escort No 1521 through Kingston on its afternoon ceremonial run. In front, RF502 shows the rather untidy appearance created by sticking posters on vacant spaces such as the roof. Trolleybus No 1521, an AEC dating from 1939, was eventually saved from the breakers and has operated at the East Anglian Transport Museum, Carlton Colville, near Lowestoft. *Geoff Rixon*

*Right:*
**Meals on wheels**
In March 1973, RTL1556 finds employment as a cafeteria for a mobile film crew, a pull-out counter having been built into the nearside downstairs saloon. The location is Mount Pleasant Road, Ealing, which, in the 20 years I lived there with my parents, had only once witnessed London buses. That occasion was when road works in nearby Woodfield Road caused a one-way diversion of route 97 past my house (the white semi on the left with the square bay window, for those interested!). *Author*

*Below right:*
**Ins and outs**
In 1960, LT purchased three new AEC Reliances (RWs) to test the concept of a separate entrance and exit on OPO vehicles to speed up passenger loading and unloading. The RWs visited several Country Area garages before being sold to Chesterfield Corporation in December 1963. RW3, pictured here at Hertford on 10 March 1963, has survived into preservation. *Hugh Ramsey*

*Above:*
**Mutilated masterpiece**
RT3745 passes the remains of London's only Moroccan-style railway station on 4 April 1974. Built for the District Railway in 1873, this bizarre building, four storeys high with twin towers and domes, was reduced to two floors by bombing in 1940 and was demolished in 1976. *R. C. Riley*

*Opposite:*
**Hybrid headache**
In 1976 LT bought 164 buses with Swedish Scania running units and British Metro-Cammell bodies and classified them as the MD class. Although these buses did not vibrate like the DMSs, problems arose with corrosion and availability of spares, with the result that in little over two years of operation, the first were taken out of service. By 1983 the class was extinct. MD65 is seen at King's Cross on 12 April 1980. *Geoff Rixon*

*Opposite:*

**Nothing ventured**
After nipping over the low wall in front of the AEC works at Southall to photograph a new RMC undergoing a brake test, the cameraman was confronted with an official who, instead of ejecting him, invited him inside the works! The result was some unique material, including this view of RM1292 and RMC1456 receiving their finishing touches on the production line.
*Geoff Rixon*

*Right:*

**Second time round**
Driver-only vehicles were used on route 216 back in 1933 but, with operation confined to buses seating no more than 20 passengers, LT allowed OPO to lapse on Central Area services in 1949. This decision may have been regretted because it was five years after the conversion of the red RFs to OPO in 1959 before agreement was reached on its reintroduction. Well-loaded RF478 approaches Hampton Court roundabout in March 1972.
*Mike Harries*

*Above:*
**Welcome guest**
An acute shortage of buses in 1948/49 arising from delays in the production of RTs prompted LT to hire 180 new Tilling Group vehicles prior to their delivery to the appropriate companies. Most were lowbridge Bristol K5Gs, but 38 highbridge examples for Eastern Counties were also hired and five were allocated to Croydon garage. One of these is seen with STL2184 and LT392 on 19 February 1949. *C. Carter*

*Opposite:*
**Spider's web**
Some intricate trolleybus wiring provides added interest to this portrait of brand-new TD904, a Hants & Dorset lowbridge K5G allocated to West Green garage. Photographed at Ley Street, Ilford on 9 April 1949, the Bristol has just over six months left on route 144 before displacement by RTWs and delivery to its rightful owner. An early postwar RT, possibly RT432, plays second fiddle on this occasion. *C. Carter*

*Opposite:*
**Change of direction**
Like so many town centres, Dorking now has a one-way system, but back in September 1968 buses were able to travel north up South Street. Picking up outside a supermarket, which is displaying long-forgotten prices in shillings and pence, is RT4741 prior to heading for West Croydon on route 414. This service originated as East Surrey route S25 in 1922 and was extended to Dorking in 1924. *Mike Harries*

*Above:*
**Wired for sound**
In 1963, 10 redundant RFs were sold to British European Airways, which fitted them with communications equipment and flashing roof lights for working airside at Heathrow. One of these vehicles was ex-Green Line coach RF256, which is seen here in September 1964 standing on a site which was shortly to become a multi-storey car park. Beyond is the Ministry of Aviation's new administration block, Building 139 (later named D'Albiac House by the British Airports Authority), where the author started his working life in 1966. *Mike Harries*

*Right:*
**Uphill struggle**
The quieter B20s went some way towards redeeming the tarnished image of the earlier Daimler Fleetlines, but the fact remains that these off-the-shelf buses were generally not suitable for London's demanding conditions. DMS2573 climbs Caterham Valley Road in August 1983.
*Jim Collins*

*Opposite:*
**Gift wrapped**
Eight Routemasters received a distinctive livery to commemorate the marriage of HRH Prince Charles and Lady Diana Spencer on 29 July 1981. The previous day saw LT using these vehicles on a special service to view the wedding decorations. RM519, the only one of the eight with non-opening front windows, enters Parliament Square.
*Geoff Rixon*

*Left:*
**Tired Titan**
The evening sunlight shows up the dented bodywork of neglected Leyland Titan RTL408 as it sets off from London Zoo in August 1965. This was a bad year for the Leylands as large numbers were replaced by new Routemasters and surplus RTs from the Country Area. *Geoff Rixon*

*Below left:*
**On borrowed time**
The take-over of LT by the Greater London Council and the surrender of the bus network outside its area led to the formation of London Country on 1 January 1970. This resulted in 413 RFs being transferred to the new company. In addition, five red RFs had been lent by the Central Area in October 1969 to cover shortages and these became hired vehicles. February 1971 saw RF388 at Crawley garage, a few weeks before its return to LT. London Country seemed reluctant to paint garage codes on these RFs, thus providing a rare opportunity to see the stencil plates which had fallen into disuse in 1961/62. *Mike Harries*

*Opposite:*
**Lost civilisation**
There is not a house in sight, let alone an estate, at the Charts Down terminus of route 449 on 12 March 1981. Taking the country air is RP31, one of a class of OPO AEC Reliances introduced in November 1971 to replace crew-operated Routemaster coaches on all Green Line services apart from the 709. However, a combination of poor reliability and a change in the Green Line image in favour of luxury coaches saw the RPs demoted to bus work by 1979. RP31 was scrapped in 1983 and the last of the class was withdrawn from public service in February 1984. *Geoff Rixon*

*Right:*
**Time warp**
The early 1960s atmosphere in this photograph contrasts with the dated appearance of trolleybus No 1 which is accentuated by the vehicle's 'as withdrawn' 1949 condition (apart from the repainted wheels). Exhumed from Clapham Museum for the ceremonial farewell run and towed back there immediately afterwards, No 1's next adventure was a visit to Aldenham Works in 1975 for refurbishment and repainting. However, it was not until 1990 that the 'Diddler', as it was nicknamed, ran once more under its own power, this time at Carlton Colville. *Geoff Rixon*

*Opposite:*
**Action replay**
The wonderful array of 'period' shop blinds may have disappeared but it is still possible to stand at this point on a summer Sunday and see a Lincoln green GS on the 433. Pictured here at Dorking in April 1968, GS42 was the last of the class to be overhauled at Aldenham and was one of the final pair in service, surviving until 31 March 1972. The circular Guildford-Dorking leisure service which today covers part of the old route is normally worked by GS13. *Mike Harries*

*Opposite:*
**Aldenham aristocrat**
The works were closed down in November 1986 despite the quality of workmanship, demonstrated here at Kingston on 17 August 1983. Metrobus M57 was painted in General livery as part of LT's Golden Jubilee celebrations. This scene has changed considerably in a comparatively short time: the stone building behind the bus has now made way for the Bentalls shopping centre and the road is pedestrianised. *Geoff Rixon*

*Above:*
**Way out**
It seems extraordinary that as late as April 1978, when this picture was taken, 30-year-old red double-deckers with conductors were still operating so far from the metropolis. RT1538 enters Downe, in Kent, only a few days before route 146 from Bromley was converted to BL operation. *Dave Brown*

*Above:*
**Blind spot**
RC12 could be going to Luton or Crawley in this view at St Albans on
9 August 1969. The 14 RC coaches introduced in November 1965 brought
higher standards of comfort to Green Line passengers, but, regrettably, lower
standards of reliability. Demoted to bus work in 1974, these vehicles were
withdrawn from passenger service by 1978. *Hugh Ramsey*

*Opposite:*
**Durban diversion**
A shortage of trolleybuses in 1941 prompted LT to purchase 43 very non-
standard vehicles originally intended for South Africa. These trolleybuses
were the first eight-feet wide vehicles in London and were given special
clearance to operate. No 1737 stands in Ilford High Road on 3 June 1950 at a
time when trolleybuses still followed the tramway practice of not carrying
depot codes. *C. Carter*

*Opposite:*
**Charmed life**
Back in the days of Police boxes and Civil Defence sirens, RM1183 was just another Routemaster standing in Walton Road, East Molesey. By 1988, it was redundant but escaped the scrapyard, thanks to Southend Transport. After five years at the seaside, fortune smiled again and RM1183 is now with London & Country at Leatherhead garage. The fact that it is the first 'short' open-platformed RM to wear Lincoln green does not detract from the pleasure of seeing this vehicle in operation. *Geoff Rixon*

*Above:*
**Return to sender**
London Country's XFs Nos 6 and 7 are back at East Grinstead after their three-year stint on the innovative 'Blue Arrow' services at Stevenage. *Jim Collins*

*Back cover:*
**Into deepest Kent**
Ex-Green Line RT4505 has the road to itself as it approaches Sevenoaks Weald on its journey from Chipstead to distant Tonbridge in September 1969. *Dave Brown*